CHOCOLAT

vol.3

JiSang Shin·Geo

WORDS FROM THE CREATORS

In the recent past, there have been a lot of tragic events in the world. The incident on the Dae-Gu Subway, the Iraq war, and things that have been happening on a personal level for us, too.

L'il Cheapskate and L'il Poopy Head lost their beloved kitty due to an unforeseen accident. Living...is never as beautiful as it looks in a drawing, but by drawing a portrait of the kitty who passed, we hope to erase a few of the painful memories.

Ha-ha...

This is the third book. For those who have been waiting for it, we hope it will be a nice gift as the season turns to Spring...

Ji-Sang Shin & Geo

Q&A
with Ji-Sang Shin and Geo

1. Which character from Chocolat is your favorite?
Ji-Sang Shin: Jin (Strangely enough, I'm attracted to him! ^ ^)
Geo: E-Soh (He's the easiest to draw… -.-;;)

2. Chocolat's most popular female heroine is Kum-Ji!
How does everyone feel about her at the studio?
We complain that for an ugly girl, she sure is lucky!
Basically, she's at rock bottom! T.T

3. Who's the hardest character to write?
E-Wan, for sure. He's definitely got a complicated personality.

4. Which character do you think is the worst to draw?
E-Wan, again…he's definitely the hardest to draw… T.T
Though he may look solid, it's easy to make mistakes
when doing that character. ^ ^;;

5. Any messages for the fans?
To all of our fans who love Chocolat…
You know we're forever in your debt, right?
E-Wan, E-Soh, Kum-Ji, Jin…Please continue to love all of them.
And 'til we meet again in volume 4, bye-bye!

IT'S ME. SHE'S ON HER WAY UP.

YEAH.

WHATEVER YOU WISH.

I'M SURE THERE'S A LOT OF PENT-UP EMOTION YOU'VE BEEN DYING TO RELEASE.

BEAT HER UP...RIP HER APART...WHATEVER DOES THE TRICK!

I'LL TAKE CARE OF THE REST AFTERWARDS!

DRIVER.

PLEASE TAKE ME TO B.S.B.

YES, MISS.

SO, KUM-JI...

YOU SHOULD BE CAREFUL WHEN TAKING CANDY FROM STRANGERS, MY DEAR...BECAUSE YOU NEVER KNOW WHAT'S IN THE WRAPPER.

HUH?

HEY, WHERE'D SHE GO?

SNIFF SNIFF

WHERE'S MY NEW NIECE...?!!

...IS WHAT HE WISHES HE COULD SAY (HE AND YOO-JUNG DATE IN SECRECY)!

E-WAN TOOK HER OUTSIDE.

DAMN IT!!

I KNEW HE WAS ACTING SUSPICIOUS!!!

MY HEAD
HURTS...

SIGH

WELL, I, GUESS
IT'S FOR THE BEST
THAT IT'S ALL
OVER. IF NOTHING
ELSE, MY WISH
CAME TRUE AND I
SAW JIN IN
PERSON...AND
THAT'S SOME-
THING.

......

BUT...
MY HEART
STILL HURTS...

E-SOH...

HE
SAID HE
LIKED ME...

YESTERDAY WAS BAD, AND TODAY DOESN'T LOOK ANY BETTER.

WHAT HAPPENED YESTERDAY JUST KEEPS REPEATING ITSELF IN MY MIND.

IT'S EXHAUSTING.

HYO-SUN...

Ding ♪ ♪ Dong

Y.ill

STILL NOT TALKING 2 HYO-SUN? *PRETTY BOY JIN*

YEP... THAT'S CORRECT...

SIGH

WHOOSH

IT'S COLD...

SNIP SNIP SNIP

IT FEELS A BIT...YOU KNOW...SINCE THE VAN IS PARKED IN THE PARKING LOT AND...I'M SNEAKING OUT THE BACK DOOR ...I JUST DON'T LIKE DECEIVING THOSE KIDS, YOU KNOW?

IF YOU GO THROUGH THE PARKING LOT, WE'LL NEVER GET OUT. DIDN'T YOU SEE THE CROWD?

WE SCHEDULED IT SO YOU'D BE RELEASED BEFORE SCHOOL GOT OUT...SO I HAVE NO IDEA HOW THEY FOUND OUT AHEAD OF TIME IN ORDER TO DITCH.

HARDCORE, HARDCORE--THESE FANS REALLY LIVE UP TO THE NAME.

THEY'LL GO THROUGH ANYTHING FOR YOU.

I COULDN'T GIVE WHAT THEY GIVE EVEN IF YOU PAID ME.

HA-HA-HA

THEY'RE COMING.

YEAH, I SEE THEM.

CUT IT, YOU TWO.

IN THE NAME OF LOVE AND JUSTICE, I SHALL PUNISH YOU!!*

YOU'RE GETTING PRETTY HARSH. WHAT'S GOING ON WITH YOU?

JUST HAVING A L'IL FUN.

*EDITOR'S NOTE: SAILOR MOON REFERENCE ^_^

I GET A CHARGE OUT OF WATCHING THESE TWO PIPSQUEAKS GET ALL SHIVERY AND MAD.

SHIVER

EUN-HEE, PLEASE TAKE THE GROUP AND GO ON AHEAD.

YEAH?

THERE'S SOMEONE I'D LIKE TO SAY HELLO TO.

DISGUSTING.

HMPH

ER...I...

IS TODAY...

...THE DAY FOR GETTING MY FEET STEPPED ON?

OHMYGAWD, IT'S THEM, IT'S THEM!!

EEEK! IT REALLY IS THEM!!

SNIFFLE

BA-
BUMP

GOOD JOB! EXCELLENT WORK!!

STICK A FORK IN IT, WE'RE DONE!

ALL RIGHT♥ IT'S FINALLY OVER!

DOES IT FEEL DAT GOOD?

ACTUALLY, IT'S A LITTLE BITTERSWEET. IT FELT MORE LIKE A DREAM THAN REALITY...

THE GOOD-BYE PARTY IS GONNA BE OFF THE HOOK, RIGHT?

IT'S GONNA BE SUPER, ULTRA, MEGA-SPECIAL, YA PUNK!

AH!

WHAT?

DON'T MAKE SUCH A BIG PRODUCTION OUT OF IT. JUST BRING SOME SPARE CLOTHES AND YOUR OWN TOOTHBRUSH OR SOMETHING.

HONESTLY? THAT'S ALL?!!

I DON'T NEED TO PACK ANYTHING?

HOW CAN THAT BE POSSIBLE?

WELL, MY LITTLE AUNTY SURE HAS GROWN INTO HER NEW ROLE.

WOW, SHE'S ACTING LIKE A TRIP TO AMERICA'S NO BIG DEAL.

AIRPORT? SWEETIE, WHAT ARE YOU TALKING ABOUT?

WHY WOULD WE NEED TO GET ON AN AIRPLANE TO GO TO BONGWHA*? IT'S JUST IN KYUNG-BOOK PROVINCE.

WHAT AIRPORT?

K-K-KYUNGBOOK...?!!

BONGWHA?!!!

WHAT ABOUT AMERICA?!!

*5 HOUR DRIVE SOUTH OF SEOUL.

TO BE CONTINUED IN CHOCOLAT VOL. 4!

Bring it on!

vol.3

Baek HyeKyung

...QUICKLY...

...I NEED
TO SHOW THAT
THERE'S NOTHING
BETWEEN ME
AND SEUNG-SUH

Danbi Original

Chocolat vol.3

Story and art by JiSang Shin · Geo

Translation Jackie Oh
English Adaptation Jamie S. Rich
Touch-up and Lettering Terri Delgado · Marshall Dillon
Graphic Design EunKyung Kim

ICE Kunion

English Adaptation Editor HyeYoung Im · J. Torres
Managing Editor Marshall Dillon
Marketing Manager Erik Ko
Senior Editor JuYoun Lee
Editorial Director MoonJung Kim
Managing Director Jackie Lee
Publisher and C.E.O. JaeKook Chun

Chocolat © 2005 JiSang Shin · Geo
First published in Korea in 2002 by SIGONGSA Co., Ltd.
English text translation rights arranged by SIGONGSA Co., Ltd.
English text © 2005 ICE KUNION

Published by ICE Kunion.
SIGONGSA 2F Yeil Bldg. 1619-4, Seocho-dong, Seocho-gu, Seoul, 137-878, Korea

ISBN : 89-527-4480-2

First printing, August 2006
10 9 8 7 6 5 4 3 2 1
Printed in Canada